THERE'S NO WAY TO DO IT WRONG!

by Gary Miller

The 7-Minute Writer
No Way to Do It Wrong!
How to Get Young Learners to Take Risks,
Tell Stories, Share Opinions, and
Fall in Love with Writing

With 101 Bonus Prompts
by Gary Miller

© 2021 Gary Miller

All rights reserved. No part of this book may be reproduced in any form or by any means without the prior written consent of the publisher, except in cases of brief quotations used in reviews and certain other noncommercial uses permitted by copyright law.

Design by Sian Foulkes

TABLE OF CONTENTS

PART I How It Works (Don't Skip This Part. It's Important!)

INTRODUCTION
What This Book Isn't (A Kind of Nutrition Label) 4

CHAPTER 1
7 Minutes Can Change Everything! 7

CHAPTER 2
Three Simple Steps 11

CHAPTER 3
The Rules 12

CHAPTER 4
Sharing 15

Part II The Prompts

CHAPTER 5
Icebreakers 18

CHAPTER 6
Opening Doors 23

CHAPTER 7
Making a Scene 29

CHAPTER 8
Can We Talk 33

CHAPTER 9
That Makes Sense 36

CHAPTER 10
Thickening a Plot 38

CHAPTER 11
It's My Story, and I'm Stickin' to It 44

CHAPTER 12
That's Just Wrong! (Or Maybe It Isn't!) 46

CHAPTER 13
Don't Just Write. Publish! 48

Part III THE BIG BONUS

101 Prompts to Use Any Way You Want! 50

THERE'S NO WAY TO DO IT WRONG!

What This Book Is and Isn't
(A Kind of Nutrition Label)

This book helps kids learn how to write, and how to love writing. But it doesn't focus on Grammar, Usage, and Mechanics (GUM). It doesn't include checklists of skills and strategies. It wasn't created to align with Texas standards, the California standards, Common Core, or the Federal Aviation Administration standards. Nor was it designed to improve test scores.
For decades, I've written textbooks and other educational materials that do all these things (well, except for the FAA standards). Frankly, I'm a bit tired of them and I think that, while they have their place, there's room for something different. Also, I found a way to teach writing that kids love, and it only takes 7 Minutes to prove it.

I created this book of to accomplish three goals:
- Get kids writing
- Convince kids that they can write successfully.
- Make writing a fun experience for all the kids who do it, so they'll become skilled, enthusiastic writers.

You can meet all these goals using simple 7-Minute Prompts. I've been using them for years, and they've produced amazing results with all sorts of groups, from middle and high school students to adults of all backgrounds. I'm pretty sure that you can produce the same great results with your students.

Oh, before I forget, I've also included some great writing tips for people of all ages. These can't be found in most books used to teach writing. But they're the tricks and insider info that professional writers all over the world use to engage, inform, and entertain their readers—and keep them coming back for more. When your students learn and practice these simple principles, their writing will really take off!

Ready to get started? It's easy! Just pick a prompt. Set the timer for 7 Minutes. And GO!

There's no way to do it wrong!

Gary

CHAPTER 1
7 Minutes Can Change Everything!

For many students, writing is a bit like parachuting from a plane: before they can feel the exhilaration, they need to take a difficult first step. That can be hard—especially if they have time to procrastinate, because that's when the voice of the internal editor creeps in.

"I'm a terrible writer."
"I'll never get this done on time."
"Writing is boring, and it's hard, too."
"I don't have anything to write about."

When this happens, the result is too often failure—and failing makes students dislike the writing process even more than they did before.

Instead, consider an alternative: give an assignment that guarantees success. Provide your students with a well-focused prompt (more on that later). Tell them they're going to write for 7 Minutes, and that the only rule is this one: **There's No Way to Do It Wrong.**

Students can write poetry or prose, a rap or a song. They can write fiction or nonfiction. They can tell their own story, someone else's, or the story of an imaginary character they just made up. They don't need to spell everything right, and no one cares if they use correct grammar or punctuation. Because **There's No Way to Do It Wrong.** (Yes, I know I just said this. I'm going to say it a lot, and so should you!)

What happens when you do this? Again, and again, students succeed. They jump right in, without the company of their fears or their internal editor. They access their imaginations and their deepest feelings. They create work that surprises and delights them, and does the same to everyone else. They learn that writing can be fun. And most important, they learn that they are writers—that they have something worth saying, and that when they communicate using the written word, good things happen.

A Word (or Two) About Long Form and "Do Later" Assignments

Of course, giving students longer or "Do Later" writing assignments is something all teachers do—because we have to. The writing standards for students include addressing fully organized long-form pieces that express an opinion, tell a story, explain a process, or inform readers about a topic. While we work on these writing forms in the classroom, we often end up sending work home for our students to do later. (Although some schools have stopped doing this altogether and employ flipped-classroom strategies in which kids do their "homework" in the classroom.) But whether done at home or at school, long-term or do-later assignments are a necessity. We won't always be around to provide direct support, so students have to learn to write at length on their own.

Still, many of us know that "Do Later" assignments can create all sorts of barriers to success by

- Distancing students from the teaching that comes before the assignment.
- Giving students a chance to explore and reinforce their fears of failure.
- Wasting any enthusiasm for writing that they have built in the classroom.
- Making students feel that they are alone with a disagreeable task.
- Making it easier for cell phones, social media, extracurricular activities, and issues at home to distract students from their work.

7-Minute Prompts: A Productive Supplement

7-Minute Prompts offer a productive supplement to "Do Later" assignments. They put students on the spot—in a good way—and force them to leap immediately into writing without worrying about whether or not they'll succeed. The instruction and the writing happen in the moment, so they stay connected.

In 7 Minutes, we can't ask students to tackle a complicated assignment. But we can invite them to leap into low-risk, fun assignments that build creativity, community, and enthusiasm for writing. As they do so, they develop the skills and self-esteem they need to take on longer projects. And since **There's No Way to Do It Wrong**, students always succeed—or maybe they just fail fast!

The Quickest Way to Fail

OK, that headline seems a little scary. I mean, do we really want students to fail—and fail quickly, at that? Surprisingly, the answer is yes. In fact, we want students to learn to get comfortable with falling short—but also with discovering the tiny successes that happen with every imperfect effort.

This sounds contradictory, but it works, and you need look no further than Silicon Valley to prove it. In software development, designers often employ a fail-fast model. Failing fast helps them avoid investing huge amounts of money and time to create a final product that might not work.

Instead, tech designers learn to fail fast. They try out a small low-risk step in the creation of the product. If that step works, great! And if it falls short, as it often does, the designers learn from that and use their knowledge to improve the next version. This exponentially increases the likelihood that their next step will be successful.

That, in a nutshell, is what makes the 7-Minute Prompt so effective. Students write short pieces, and they know up front that in 7 Minutes no one can produce perfect work. So instead of looking for shortcomings, we look for progress. It's low risk and high reward!

What About Grading?

We recommend that you don't grade 7-Minute Prompts, but they are perfect for collecting in student portfolios. You can employ them very effectively to assess student understanding and progress over time. And through peer sharing and positive feedback, students can learn how to make their writing even stronger. (More on that in the next chapter!)

A Note On Second Language Learners

7-Minute Prompts can work great with Second Language Learners, and help build their love of writing and speaking in English. But they may need a little support to help them succeed, One great strategy is to provide them with oral examples of responses before they write. Another is to allow them to give their responses orally before writing them down. Since there is No Way to Do It Wrong, they can only succeed!

CHAPTER 2
Three Simple Steps

In application, the process involves three simple steps: a well-focused writing prompt; 7 Minutes to write on any topic they want; and a sharing session in which students read their work aloud and offer comments on each other's writing. It's just that simple.

Step 1 Prompt

Just pick one of our handy-dandy prompts. Then share it. You can do this however you like. Write the prompt on a whiteboard. Send it by telegram or carrier pigeon. Or simply read it out loud. Ask students to write it down.

(If you choose, you can toss out some ideas about where the prompt might take your students. You might also read a sample response to the prompt from a previous workshop. But it's my experience that you get a better diversity of results and have more fun if you let students take the prompt wherever they are inspired to take it.)

Step 2 Write

Set your timer for 7 Minutes and holler "Go!"
Don't show students the timer, as that can prove distracting. I usually let people know when there is one minute left to write. As students get used to the process, this aspect will become easier. They simply write until the timer goes off.

Step 3 Share

Invite students to read their work aloud. After a student reads, invite comments. (But there are some rules! You can find out more in—you guessed it—the next chapter!)

CHAPTER 3
The Rules

7-Minute Prompts are designed to allow for maximum freedom and creativity. I want students to view writing as an endless roadmap of possibility, not a one-way street. That's why when it comes to using 7-Minute Prompts, there are only...

TWO RULES!

Rule 1: There is no way to do this wrong.

Have you heard this before? I know you have. This is a statement that encourages students to go forth boldly, to take chances, and to proceed with confidence. Remember, you're not looking for perfect spelling, perfect grammar, perfect ideas, or perfect chains of logic. You ARE looking for the creative employment of all sorts of writing techniques, from description and dialogue to storytelling and sense of place. The goals are for kids to have fun and learn to love writing.

> The goal is to learn from experience, not write to perfection.

Rule 2: All comments must be positive and supportive

It's important to all writers—and particularly to beginning writers—that criticism of their work takes the form of constructive comments. In 7-Minute Writes, it's important to focus ONLY on what students are doing right, without pointing out the elements that need improvement.

Now, this stands at odds with the traditional idea of "correcting" a paper, or even of providing traditional writing critiques. So why am I suggesting that you teach this way? Because I've found that a "positive only" approach to sharing increases students' willingness to write and share. But that doesn't mean students aren't learning how to improve their writing. In any given sharing session, they not only uncover their own strengths, but those of their peers. Your job is to point out that students can improve their writing by focusing on what they do well, and through observing, learning, and employing techniques other students use effectively.

About Sharing

The sharing of writing is where the magic happens. It's when students get to see the impact of their work on a receptive audience. It's when they discover that they can use writing to inform, to entertain, to provoke, to tell a story. But in order to make the sharing effective, you need to do it right.

(Fill in the blank to find out how. Read the next _____!)

CHAPTER 4
Sharing

Sharing the results of a prompt may be the most fun part of 7-Minute Prompts. You and your students will be consistently amazed by the amount of creativity, humor, insight, and personality that can be packed into just a few minutes of writing. You'll laugh hysterically, you'll be swept up by emotion, and you'll immerse yourself in some of the most heartfelt writing you have ever heard read aloud.

What's the best thing about sharing? In our experience, it's hearing the broad variety of responses from a group of students given the exact same prompt. There's a reason for that. Often, we ask students to do general writing assignments, but topic choice is up to them.

For example, we may ask them to "write about a time when you learned something about yourself." When presented with such a prompt, students may have a hard time coming up with a good idea. Also, they know what kind of response you are looking for, but they might not know how to produce it. Particularly for those who have a hard time with writing, this can be scary. And the results may be kind of, well, general. But when all students write from a carefully positioned prompt* and **There's No Way to Do It Wrong**, imaginations are set free and you get a true sample of the creativity and different perspectives of the entire group. Students find this thrilling—and teachers do, too.

Of course, in order to make sharing effective, students will need some guidelines. I do have a few, and they're listed below. (But I don't call them rules, because that would mean there are more than two!)

---

*(What in tarnation is a positioned prompt? And why are positioned prompts important? You'll find out in Chapter 6)

Sharing is Voluntary

It might seem backward to let students know right from the start that they are not required to share. But oddly enough, I've found that it seems to make some students more likely to share. And it's also my experience that very few students can resist the temptation to share in an atmosphere in which ALL feedback is positive feedback.

Respectful Listening is Mandatory

In order for literary readings to work, the audience needs to listen both attentively and respectfully. This is critically important when the works read are short—as the products of 7-Minute Prompts are likely to be.

I've found that saying right before the sharing that each student has worked hard on his or her piece and deserves attention can be a really helpful way to create focus. I also stress that it's important to let the reader know you are listening, by focusing on the reader with your eyes.

All Feedback Must Be Positive

Once again, the goal is POSITIVE feedback. Letting a student know what they are doing right not only reinforces that student's writing, but provides examples and ideas for other students. It's a win-win.

Some Great Ideas for Sharing

- Ask the author to read aloud.
- Ask one person to read the work of another author. This is very helpful if people are shy about reading aloud.
- Encourage students to perform their work. (Of course, this works particularly well with dialogue pieces or scripts written for plays, radio, TV, or film.)
- Give EVERYONE who reads their work a BIG round of applause.

Writing and Sharing Your Own Work

As teachers, we don't usually write and share our own work in the classroom. But I've found that this can be incredibly helpful to students. Surprisingly, it's not always because your writing will set a good example of craft. Students appreciate seeing that their teachers struggle to get their words right, that they'll go out on a limb emotionally to speak some truth, and that they can write something that's not so polished but could be polished later.

CHAPTER 5
Icebreakers

For your first 7-Minute Prompt session, it's a good idea to make the leap as small as possible by giving students a prompt they can relate to. Often, a great way to start is to ask students to write about themselves. This not only provides a comfortable subject area for students to address, but it can also help to build bonds in the group as students become aware of common interests and backgrounds and begin to find their voices in the group.

"Where I'm From": A Foolproof Way to Start

Particularly if you are piloting a new writing group, it's important to get students off to a good start by providing a prompt for which nearly anyone can experience success. George Ella Lyons' poem "Where I'm From" has inspired countless student poems, many of which are truly remarkable. These poems start with the phrase "I am from," and proceed to describe the writer's family history or home in creative ways.

Often, the poems take the form of a list. Here's one such poem (opposite), written by a student from one of my workshops. You might want to share this example with your students before they begin writing.

The great gift of "I Am From" is twofold.

1) ACCESSIBILITY
"I Am From" poems are poems everyone can relate to, and everyone can write. Each person is from somewhere, and each has a unique story to tell.

2) CONNECTION
It helps students bond over common (and uncommon) backgrounds and interests. When students listen to a peer's "I Am From" poem, they get to know that peer in a whole new way. This helps bring the group together.

"I Am From"
by E

I am from the dark emerald of the evergreen trees
    swaying like dancers in the wind.
    From the dark red cherry wood cabinets,
    the smell of bacon sizzling on a hot griddle
    waking me up and prompting me to come downstairs.
    I am from my tree house, sitting in the ninety-foot-tall white pine,
    its bark like the scarred hide of an ancient tortoise.

I am from my orange bean bag chair
    that was custom made and says "God of the Universe" in bold letters.
    I am from old dogs and soft blue sheets,
    sitting in a secluded room listening to music.

I am from cheese toast and maple cappuccinos
    starting off the day.
    From savory beef bourguignon
    cooked on a small black stove.
    I am from linguine with clam sauce
    but no cheese! You'll ruin it!

I am from "Give me fourteen nanoseconds!"
    and "Vacuum your room—or else."
    From my father's strong hand, hardworking
    and my mother, kind, considerate.
    I am from legions
    migrating across the sea from Poland and Sicily.
    I am from here,
    smalltown Vermont.
    From this house and its people
    changed by each other,
    changing each other.
    I am from everywhere
    and nowhere,
    from right here,
    and right now.

Time to Write!!

- Share the "I Am From" poem, and talk about its characteristics—it's used to tell about a person's background. Remind students that "I Am From" poems often use listing as a technique.

- Tell students they are going to write a poem called "I Am From." Set a timer for 7 minutes.

- Holler "Go!" and start the timer.

- When time is up, ask students to share.

Helpful Hints

- Just write. Don't edit yourself.
- Don't worry about whether the final product will be perfect
- **There is no way you can do this wrong.**

More Icebreaker Prompts

Here are some more icebreaker prompts in the style of "Where I'm From." Some address biography more concretely, and some more abstractly.
"I am the one who …"

- "Some good advice from the true me …"
- "The safest place on Earth …"
- "If I were in charge …"
- "What they should know about the real me …"
- "I am the only one who sees …"
- "When no one is looking …"
- "I can always count on _____ …"
- "I couldn't live without _____ …"
- "The secret goal of my life …"
- "I'm a big fan of …"
- "In my secret heart …"
- "Did I ever tell you …"
- "Let me introduce myself …"
- "I'm a little bit shy, but …"
- "I'm so glad to meet you …"
- "Hey! I didn't see you there …"
- "If you just listen, I'll tell you …"
- "When I was little …"
- "My friends always say …"
- "What you might not know about me is …"

> "First sentences are doors to worlds."
>
> —Ursula K. LeGuin

CHAPTER 6
Opening Doors

You may have heard that first sentences are designed to "hook" the reader, and to make the reader want to read more. That is undoubtedly true—especially in a time when more and more voices, from books and magazines to blogs and tweets, are vying for readers' attention. You have probably experienced the thrill of a first sentence that is simply impossible to resist. And you've seen your students equally thrilled when a great first sentence draws them into reading a longer work.

As teachers, we often think of first sentences as doors that welcome readers in. What we don't consider as often is the power of first sentences to **welcome writers in—to help them start writing and keep writing**.

To understand why first sentences are important to writers, and how they work, let's consider another quote, this time by writer Margaret Atwood: "The fact is that blank pages inspire me with terror. What will I put on them? Will it be good enough?"

That's exactly the feeling that many students have when confronted with a traditional assignment or writing prompt. They are asked, for example, to write a story about an experience they had, to express their opinion about a public issue, or to describe a person, place, or thing. But their first job is to write an opening sentence. And for many kids, this process can stop them cold.

For that reason, it can be helpful to do something to make the process easier: to open the door by providing students with a great first sentence.

Of course, our eventual goal is to teach students to write great first sentences on their own. But giving them some first sentences accomplishes two critical steps toward that goal. It gives them some great examples of engaging, powerful first sentences. And it helps them to experience for themselves the power of first sentences to inspire great writing.

Writing from a Given First Sentence

Ask students to write for 7 Minutes from one of the first-sentence prompts below. Remember, it's not important for students to reach the end of the story.

- Carlos wanted to bring the dog home, but Ana completely disagreed.
- There's only one way to clean your bedroom.
- If you want to be the best at your sport, here's what you need to do.
- The train car suddenly went dark…
- I had never done anything like that before.
- I met a ghost last night.
- Here's why clean energy works for everybody.
- As the playoffs approached, the girls all agreed that beating East Side would probably be a breeze, but there was something they didn't count on.
- It was the first time I had ever really looked at the house.
- It was only quarter past seven, and already the kids were driving her crazy.
- At the bottom of their problems was that fact that Sammy hated work more than anything else he could think of.
- Here's why _____ is a completely terrible movie.
- Frog wanted to stay friends with Bunny forever, but lately Bunny had been acting like a total jerk.
- Clarissa had been sick for more than a week, but there was no money for a doctor.
- By the time Caroline arrived, Lena was ready to go home, but Caroline had other plans.

Time to Write!!

1 Talk about the characteristics of good first sentences: they open a new world or signal an opportunity for the reader to learn or be entertained. Often, they include one or more of the following: a character, a desire, and an obstacle or opposing force.

2 Have students write their own first sentences. Ask them to use the following checklist to make sure they include important elements in the sentence:

- ✓ Open a new world
- ✓ Opportunity for Learning or Entertainment
- ✓ A Character
- ✓ A Desire
- ✓ An obstacle or opposing force

3 Holler "go!" and start the timer.

4 When time is up, ask students to share their first sentences.

Positioned Prompts

Most conventional writing prompts ask students to choose their own topic, make up their own position, or state their own perspective. That's because one goal of teaching is to enable students to do these things independently. But doing so also sets many students up for a struggle. What do I want to write about? What do I want to say? What tone or position should I take? In contrast, many of my 7-Minute Prompts provide a bit of momentum. The door has been opened a crack so students can move into a new world with ease. I like to call prompts that set the stage for the student in this way **positioned prompts**.

Positioned prompts don't always need to include a character, a desire, and an obstacle. But what they DO need to do is to open up a world for writers to venture into.

To better understand how this works, let's compare some examples of non-positioned and positioned prompts.

NON-POSITIONED PROMPT
"Write a poem about your background. Tell readers about where you are from, and who your family members are. Give examples of special family traditions, events, and times."

POSITIONED PROMPT
"I Am From…"

NON-POSITIONED
Think about the last time you attended a family or community event. Be sure to include a detailed description of the event, including sights, sounds, smells, and how the event made you feel.

POSITIONED
When Helen entered the fairground, what she saw, heard, and felt dazzled her senses.

NON-POSITIONED
Try to recall a time when something unexpected happened. Write about what happened, and organize the events in order so your reader can experience it with you. Be sure to include lots of sensory details.

POSITIONED
Let me tell you about the time my day did NOT turn out as planned.

NON-POSITIONED
Write a composition in which you explain how to make something. You might write about a food item, a handcrafted item, or anything else that you know how to make. Be sure to clearly explain each step in the process so that a reader could make the item the way you do.

POSITIONED
Here's how you make the World's Most Legendary Sandwich.

NON-POSITIONED
Who is the person from history that you would most like to meet and talk to? Why?

POSITIONED
Believe it or not, I met Eleanor Roosevelt at the convenience store.

CHAPTER 7
Making a Scene

Scenes create a pathway from the start of the story to its finish, but the direction of the path is always changing. Each scene is a step. Sometimes a scene leads a person closer to his or her desire. Sometimes the path leads farther away. Sometimes it does neither.

At the start of a scene, a character wants something. An obstacle stands in the way.

So What's a Scene?

In general, a scene is a brief dramatic interaction between two or more characters. In that interaction, the characters act on their desires. The main character tries to get what they want. Other characters oppose this desire, because they want something different.

At the end of the scene, the main character has done one of three things:

Taken a step closer to what they desire.

Taken a step away from what they want. In this case, there is a setback, and the character is farther away from they desire than at the start of the scene.

Moved neither toward nor away from the desire. In this case, there is a stalemate. But the main character won't give up, and will try again.

For example, imagine a story in which the character's main desire is to prove to his parents that he is capable of moving out and making a living on his own. Here's how a sequence of scenes might work in the story.

In Scene 1, Aaron talks with his parents. His desire is to move out of the house. He explains that he wants to move at the end of the month, and asks them to loan him money to do so. He gives all the reasons he wants to be independent and all the things he will do: find a job, pay his own rent and bills, and pay his parents back.

The parents talk, too, acting upon a different desire. They want to stop Aaron—or at least slow him down. At first, they say they won't help him. They explain their reasoning: good jobs are hard to find, apartments cost money, and lots of little expenses can add up.

In the end, Aaron convinces them to let him try, on the condition that he gets a job and saves enough money for three months' expenses before he moves out.

In the course of a scene, two opposing desires have clashed against each other. And by the end, the characters on either side have given in a little. Aaron agrees to work so he doesn't have to borrow money. His parents agree to let him move out on his own. Aaron has taken a step **toward** what he wants. That small step is a scene.

Let's imagine the next scene in the sequence.

In Scene 2, Aaron goes to his first job interview. He faces a skeptical store owner, and tries to convince him that he would make a great salesman. Aaron makes his best pitch, but the store owner says Aaron doesn't have enough experience.

In this scene, Aaron has taken a step away from his goal (or, in a sense, stayed in the same place). Once again, opposing desires drive the scene. Aaron wants a job. The store owner wants an experienced salesperson.

In Scene 3, Aaron starts up his own microbusiness: a carwash and detailing business in his parents' garage. He convinces one neighbor to get his car washed and detailed, and the ball is rolling. By the end of the day, he has made $160.00. He has moved another step closer to his goal.

In Scene 4, the carwash gets shut down because a neighbor complains about vehicle traffic and water use. A step away from the goal.

You can see how this progression works. **Step by step, scene by scene, we learn whether a character will ultimately get what they want.**

SCENE PROMPTS

- It was almost the end of the day, and Leitha was determined to sell one more car.
- Ellen decided then and there that she and Robert would buy the house.
- "Come on!" she said. "Why won't you and your friends take me to the movie, too?"
- The burger was cooked wrong, and he was going to let the manager know it.
- Ariel needed a quarter for the subway, and she needed to get home.
- She wanted to see the show, but she didn't have a ticket.
- He had to make them understand he was telling the truth.
- If only his parents would let him get the car.
- A simple glass of water would change everything.
- He needed to tell Evelyn how he felt.
- I wanted them to hear what I had to say.
- He was being accused of stealing from the cash register, and he didn't know why.
- Everyone expected Mara to stay quiet, but she needed to speak up.
- I knew that if they didn't stop now, they'd be in big trouble.
- They say if you want something, just ask. So I did.

CHAPTER 8
Can We Talk?

Often when writers think about dialogue, they focus on trying to sound realistic. If the character is a tough guy from New Jersey, his speech should be tough, too. If she's a sophisticated diplomat educated at high-end private schools, then her speech should sound quite different from a character who was raised on a farm in rural West Virginia. While this is 100 percent correct, it is critical to remember that dialogue is more than just talk.

So what else does dialogue have to do? It needs to create drama and move the plot forward. In fact, dialogue is one of the prime ways in which characters express their desires. And those desires often clash. If you think this sounds a lot like how scenes work in general, you're right. In fact, dialogue is one of the ways in which drama progresses in a scene.

How Dialogue Creates Drama

In a scene, dialogue creates drama. But drama ALSO creates great dialogue. In fact, when people in a scene talk and behave in a generally agreeable fashion, when they answer each other's questions and communicate effectively, the reader will quickly get bored. Let's look at some simple examples of how it works.

EXAMPLE 1: AGREEMENT IN DIALOGUE
Melissa got home at around 6 and found Cyrus in the kitchen.

> "Hey, Cy, did you get the grocery shopping done?" she asked.
> "Yep," Cyrus said. "No problem."
> "Thanks, sweetie," Melissa said. "I really appreciate your help."

EXAMPLE 2: DISAGREEMENT

Melissa got home at around 6 and found Cyrus in the kitchen.

"Hey, Cy, did you get the grocery shopping done?" she asked.
"Sure. You try getting the grocery shopping done when you're sick as a dog and you have to fix a leaky pipe just so we can wash the dishes tonight."
Melissa slammed her purse down on the table. "That pipe has been leaking for a year," she said. "And you decide it needs fixed on the night my boss is coming for dinner?"

Now, these examples are pretty simple (and pretty obvious), but I think you'll agree that the second one is much more dramatic. Because when it comes to good dialogue, people don't often agree or communicate well. In fact, in her writing exercise book *What If*, the fantastic short story writer and writing teacher Pamela Painter has called dialogue "not quite a fight." That's as true as it gets.

Dialogue Prompts

- "Excuse me," Rennie said. "The sign says 'No Cell Phones,' but I need to call my Mom."
- "I'm sorry, but you're not allowed in here."
- "I hope you'll understand why I'm late."
- Lu cleared her throat. "You won't believe what happened to Michael at school today," she said.
- "Luke," Mom said. "Why haven't you cleaned your room?"
- "I'm having a hard time understanding why you want the job."
- "You didn't buy my land," he said. "You stole it."
- "So just exactly how did this get broken? I need to know."
- "I'll give you five thousand dollars for the car, but not a penny more," Alec said.
- "If you put me on the team, you will never regret it," Heloise said.

Understand Dialogue: It's TV Time!

A great way to understand how scenes work is to watch scenes in movies or TV shows, or read scripts of the same. When students do this, they learn how good writers use dialogue strategies to keep scenes interesting and keep viewers watching. Pre-screen some TV or streaming comedies or dramas to find some with short scenes that employ dialogue. Watch them with students and invite them to talk about how dialog works.

CHAPTER 9
That Makes Sense

Every reader knows the experience of sinking completely and effortlessly into another world. Description usually plays a big role in bringing that world to life. That's why readers respond so well to good description.

Often, people think that writers are born with a set of skills that help them succeed. But the truth is that, while natural talent does play a role, all writers need to learn new skills and practice them if they want to be successful.

What's the secret to writing great description?

Use ALL the senses, not just sight.

Of course, there's a reason that many beginning writers tend to emphasize the visual. People with vision tend to rely on it to interpret an incredible amount of information. They use vision to help them judge whether a new person we meet is friendly and whether or not it's likely to rain. They use it to judge whether food is cooked, clothes are clean, and roads are hazardous. From the moment they open their eyes in the morning to the moment they shut them at night, vision helps them perform countless tasks.

But as writers (and as people), we need to remember that our other senses are critical, too. In fact, those of us who use alarm clocks employ hearing before vision almost every morning. And as we progress through the day, we smell our food, taste our meals, and listen to the sounds of people, machines, and animals. We feel the warmth of the sun, the chill of a breeze, our clothes against our skin, the touch of a friend's hand on our own.

All Senses On Board!

Ask a group of students to write a description of the place they grew up in, a place they saw on vacation, or someone they know well, and chances are the results will rely heavily on the visual. That's natural, as vision plays such a key role in the way most people experience the world. But there is more to our sensory system. We can hear the sounds of wind blowing, smell our grandmother's cooking, feel the roughness of the boards on the side of a childhood home, taste dirt from the flower garden on our fingertips. The best descriptions employ all the senses, not just sight.

What's the best way to get students to put more of the senses into their writing? Ask—then give them a checklist to keep track.

Handy Student Checklist: The Senses—Use 'em All!

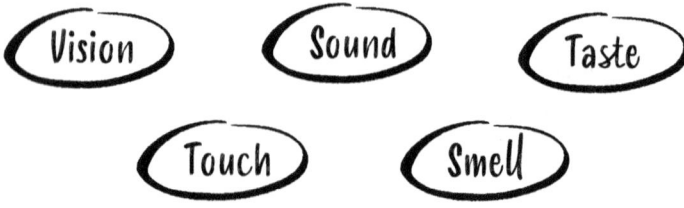

It's Practice Time!

Here are some prompts to get students started with some fun descriptive writing. Each prompt hints at one sense. Have students add as many of the others as they can.

- **When she switched on the light, she couldn't believe what she saw.**
- **The summer evening felt just perfect.**
- **The scent brought back memories.**
- **The storm got louder as it approached.**
- **The first thing she tasted was garlic.**

CHAPTER 10
Thickening a Plot

Every story needs a plot, whether it's a personal narrative or a piece of fiction. Sometimes it can be hard for students to understand what a plot is. That's because we've mostly been teaching it wrong. Most often, we talk about plot as a character, a conflict, and a resolution, which isn't entirely accurate. This can cause students to write stories that just don't work.

One reason student stories fail is that kids often understand CONFLICT as something that "happens to" a character. This CAN be the case. But thinking about plot in this way often leads to a couple of ineffective solutions. The first is a story in which a violent conflict comes out of nowhere and goes nowhere, except for a battle that quickly ends with a less than satisfying resolution. The second is a story in which a character wanders without direction until they get hit by a car, a brick, a lightning bolt, or some other disaster. If you're familiar with these two types of student stories, you are probably, well, a teacher. Because in the classroom, such stories appear all the time.

If you want your students to create stories with compelling and convincing plots, try asking your students to develop a plot using not character and conflict, but out of character and **desire**. Because that's the backbone of all great stories: a character who wants something, and wants it badly.

In *Esperanza Rising*, Esperanza wants to make a new life in a new place.
In *Hatchet*, Brian wants to survive being stranded in the alaskan wilderness.
In *The Hunger Games*, Katniss Everdeen wants to save her sister's life, and her own.
In *Huckleberry Finn*, Huck wants to escape his violent father.
In the Harry Potter series, Harry wants to protect his friends and defeat Voldemort.
In *The Lightning Thief*, Percy Jackson wants to retrieve Zeus' stolen Lightning bolt.
In *Roll of Thunder, Hear My Cry*, the Logans want to survive and hold onto their land.

So what about CONFLICT?

The conflict happens naturally, as in life, when something stands in the way of a character's desire. But calling it an **obstacle** instead of a conflict will help young writers understand something important: stories are about overcoming obstacles, which doesn't necessarily mean a space shootout or a fist fight.

What are the obstacles in each of the above cases?

- In *Esperanza Rising*, obstacles include poverty and difficult jobs.
- In *Hatchet*, obstacles include weather, animals, and a lack of tools.
- In *The Hunger Games*, obstacles include the other participants and the forces of the Capitol.
- In *Huckleberry Finn*, obstacles include the people who are looking for Huck and Jim, the people they meet along the way, and the Mississippi River itself.
- In the Harry Potter stories, the obstacles include Voldemort and his allies as well as the lack of skills and knowledge of Harry and his friends.
- In *The Lightning Thief*, obstacles include terrible monsters and manipulative gods.
- In *Roll of Thunder, Hear My Cry*, the obstacle is racism and the people who practice it.

So what is a plot?

- A Character
- A Desire
- An Obstacle (or more than one)
- A series of scenes in which the character works to get past the obstacle(s) and get what they want.

7 Minutes of Fun: The Plot Generator!

Writers sometimes come up with plots on their own. They may make up plots based on real events they know about. Or they can use a handy-dandy PLOT GENERATOR to get the job done. Here's a plot generator you can use in your own class. The Plot Generator involves four simple steps.

Step 1: Choose a Main Character

Step 2: Choose a Desire

Step 3: Choose an Obstacle

Step 4: Set the timer for 7 Minutes. Holler "Go!"

Use the list of characters, desires, and obstacles on the next page and give it a try!

MAIN CHARACTERS
Bob "The Mole" Mervyn
Ann Marie Carter-Lee O'Brien
Emilia Rodriguez
Loper Harland
Big Stevie Walker
Aaron Clements Rice
Velma Yee
Louis "Mac" Caroni
Karl Jan Karlsson
James James James

DESIRES
To win the World Series of Poker
To make the soccer team
To win the heart of the person they love
To stop the extinction of the dodo by going back in time
To give his/her hamster a good funeral
To get to school on time
To get out of detention
To convince his/her parents to get a dog

OBSTACLES
A huge snowstorm
A lack of confidence
Not enough money
A person who disagrees
The laws of physics
An escaped lion
Chronic insomnia
Someone who won't stop talking

Time to Write!!

1. Type or print a list of characters, a list of desires and a list of obstacles. Use the suggestions above or create your own. Cut each list up with scissors to create a group of character slips, a group of desire slips, and a group of obstacle slips. Put each group into a small container.

2. Invite each student to choose one character, one desire, and one obstacle at random.

   Ask each student to write the opening of a story in which the character tries to overcome the obstacle to get what they desire.

   Start with these opening sentences:

   More than anything in the world, ‹character› wanted to ‹desire›. Unfortunately, ‹obstacle› stood in the way.

3. Holler "Go!" and start the timer.

4. When time is up, ask students to share.

Keep Going!

Remember that it's really hard to write a complete story in 7 Minutes. But whether you write a sentence, a paragraph, or a page during that time, you're off and running! Invite students to take what they've written in 7 Minutes and continue to write. They can even email their extended stories to you for posting on your classroom blog.

Another Try

Once students have used the Plot Generator to start a story, have each student draw a set of character, desire, and obstacle slips or generate a character, a desire, and an obstacle on their own. Then ask students to create a story plot and opening of their own in a 7-Minute Write.

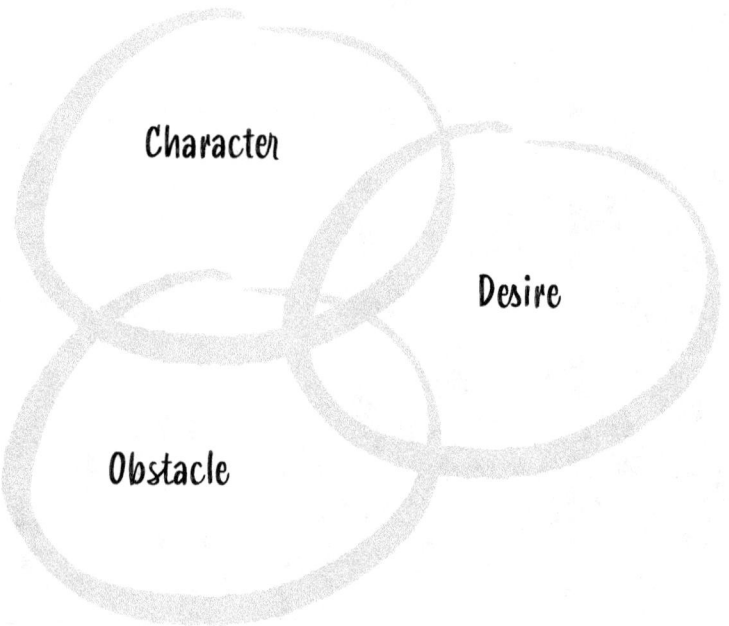

CHAPTER 11
It's My Story, and I'm Stickin' to It!

Now that students have experimented with fictional plots using the Plot Generator, it's time for them to generate stories about their own lives and write a personal narrative. The good news is that the steps are the exactly same.

1) **Choose a Main Character**. That's easy! The main character is the student doing the writing.

2) **Choose a desire**. That's easy, too. Most students have been in countless situations where they wanted to achieve a goal. Maybe it was to make the lacrosse team or to learn to play a musical instrument. Maybe it was to get a dog, cook a meal, learn to skateboard, win an argument, or build a treehouse. Ask students to choose one and write it down.

3) **Choose an obstacle**. In every case in which people try to accomplish a goal, something stands in the way. To meet their goal, students may have had to take a risk, make some money, or learn a new skill. Usually, there is more than one obstacle. Invite students to write down one major obstacle that stood in the way of their desire.

Once students have chosen a desire and an obstacle, then give them an opening prompt. And it's important to remind them that they don't have to tell a story in which they succeeded. Often times, falling short of a goal makes for a great story, and can teach some lessons, too.

Here are some great prompts for a personal narrative.

- I never thought I'd be able to _____. Here's how I did it.
- Let me tell you the story of how I _____.
- You won't believe what I had to do to make my dream of __ come true.
- In the end, ____ was a lot harder than I thought it would be.
- Nobody thought I could ever _____, but I proved them wrong.
- It seemed almost impossible, but I managed to do it.
- What started out as a great idea ended in disaster.
- Here's why it's OK to do it wrong the first time.
- Everyone said it wasn't possible.
- How did I ever get into this mess, I wondered.
- The truth was, I really wanted to quit.
- To be honest, failure can teach you a lot.

CHAPTER 12
That's Just Wrong! (Or Maybe It Isn't)

Writing 7-Minute Opinions

It's important to be able to express an opinion in writing. But doing so effectively takes a lot of practice. When students practice expressing opinions using a 7-Minute Prompt, they use the fail-fast model to quickly discover what works (and what doesn't) to enhance their writing game.

As many of your students probably know, writing an opinion piece involves naming reasons and providing supporting evidence. Refresh students' memories about this before giving them a prompt. Remind them that There's No Way to Do It Wrong, then set the timer for 7 Minutes, push the start button, and holler "Go!"

When you review 7-Minute opinions, be sure to follow the only rule for comments: All Comments Must Be Positive and Supportive. It's about identifying what students are doing right, whether it's choosing a great topic, stating some good reasons, supporting those reasons with evidence, or providing emotional impact. And don't forget that opinion pieces can have a sense of humor, too!

Here's a great list of 7-Minute Prompts for opinion pieces.

- If you want the world to be better ...
- Here's what I think ...
- I can't believe they ...
- Here's the best idea I've heard in a while ...
- I don't understand why people ...
- I'm not the only one who thinks ...
- I totally disagree with ...
- _____ is a great idea, and here's why ...
- _____ isn't as great an idea as people think. Let me prove it ...
- If you ask me, ...

CHAPTER 13
Don't Just Write. Publish!

From the first time I worked with students to publish an in-house magazine at the Rumney School in Middlesex, VT, I've witnessed the power of publishing again and again. Publishing takes student writing from the realm of just another assignment to a place where young writers can show off their writing to the world. And when that happens, you can turn even reluctant writers into motivated, enthusiastic ones.

Students can (and do) produce some great writing using 7-Minute Prompts. And you can definitely publish these pieces after a quick polish to check spelling, grammar, etc. But publishing also allow students time to revise and/or more completely develop their poems, opinions, memoirs, and stories. Whichever way you go, I promise you that when you publish your students' work, the in-class enthusiasm meter is going to hit 11.

Here are some quick ideas to get you started.

Try a Classroom Zine

Way back in the last century, young people invented zines. Short for "magazines," zines harnessed the expressive power of newsstand magazines, and did so with simple equipment and without big publishing budgets. Zines were often laid out by hand or on a desktop computer, printed at home or photocopied, and stapled together. Many were black-and-white, and sometimes they didn't include any pictures at all. Yet zines attracted millions of followers, and they taught young people everywhere two important lessons: Writing matters. And so does your voice.

Build a Blog

Easy to set up using templates offered by online blogging sites such as Squarespace, Wix, and WordPress, blogs offer a fantastic, inexpensive way to publish student work and share it with the world. Most services offer some sort of free account, but even paid accounts are relatively inexpensive. So set up an account and get publishing! Templates make it easy to insert writing and photos or other images created by students. Chances are, it will be easy to find students who already know how to use the technology. And even if you can't, video tutorials and onsite FAQs make it easy to create a blog of your own.

Publish a Book

Believe it or not, publishing a book of student work is easier than you think. Web-based book design templates and print-on-demand technology make it possible for you and your students to design and publish books for as little as a few dollars per copy. A few of the biggest names in the on-demand business are Amazon's Kindle Direct Publishing, Lulu, and BookBaby, which provide you with the tools to design, print, and order books or to create electronic books that can be posted on a website for free or paid download.

Granted, publishing a book is a bit harder than making a photocopied zine. But you likely have skilled tech allies sitting in your classroom. Invite them to create an editorial and publishing team. You might even invite some parents or members of the community to join in. I've done this a number of times, and I can assure you that the smiles you get when you open a box of your students' own published books will be authentic and long-lasting. And so will the confidence and the willingness to tackle new writing tasks with enthusiasm.

Bonus Prompts:

I hope you and your students have enjoyed learning how to use 7-Minute Prompts. And I hope you'll continue to use them! That's why I'm giving you these 101 Bonus prompts to use these any way you want! Use them any time, to help your young writers develop their skills, build their enthusiasm, or just have fun!

I've been trying to tell you …

Mickey just wanted a chance …

What I've been thinking …

Why don't you do it this way?

Take some time and think about it first …

If you want to avoid problems, …

It just didn't seem to be working …

Hardly anyone believed she could do it …

"I've got an idea, but it's a little risky," Anna said …

I just couldn't believe what I saw …

At first, it seemed pretty easy …

Things were definitely not turning out as planned …

Here's how we can solve the problem …

At just after 10, an ancient dog walked into the room …

Ask me. I know.

The supermarket had never flooded before.

The problem was, he couldn't seem to convince them of the truth.

"I don't think you understand what I mean," Tee said.

The day started out perfectly, but …

I knocked on the door hoping that no one would answer …

Here is a story I have never told anyone.

If you want to understand me, you have to …

First, I should introduce myself.

You won't believe what happened at the post office.

Can I ask you a question?

There is no way you can know what I'm feeling ...

"Things got a little out of control," Fergus said.

When the wind picks up and the rain starts to fall, I ...

It was her chance to prove herself, and she was going to give it everything she had...

He had never seen a house quite like this one ...

The secret to making friends is to ...

When I am in my favorite place ...

Here's why no one can stop me now.

Just give me a minute...

Every time I think about that summer ...

Here's the real reason I didn't go to the movies.

The door was already open, so why not?

They told me, but of course I didn't listen.

At the top of the stairs, it was quiet ...

It seemed impossible, but I needed to get the job done.

One path seemed more interesting, so I took it.

I watched the car cruise by slowly.

He found the blue envelope on a bench near the bus stop.

The neighbor won't leave us alone about that skunk.

Here is the honest truth.

After what happened, I am never doing laundry again.

Just when she thought it was over ...

After the crowds went home, the zoo was different ...

At any moment, he expected that someone would find him ...

Bonus Prompts:

Have you ever thought about why we are here?

I found an unexpected package sitting beside my door ...

Here is all it takes ...

When I woke up, I saw that the lake had frozen over ...

"Why don't you want to answer my question?" he said ...

From the top of the mountain, we could see ...

OK. Here's where I think you are wrong ...

It wasn't as bad as it looked ...

Everything started when ...

The room smelled like the inside of a tree.

It took only a few minutes ...

I felt defeated, but I decided to try again.

What could possibly go wrong?

The knight pointed his lance toward the target.

The kitchen was a mess ...

The stadium was completely silent.

Being a friend means ...

If you want to win, you need to ...

I don't know how I got the idea ...

What adults need to know about us ...

There was a bat in the closet.

If you want to make all of our lives easier ...

The first time I ever flew ...

I learned something really important when ...

Something I said that I wish I could take back ...

For the 100th time ...

Here's what I want to remember ...

"Whatever you do, don't tell anyone."

If you think you have failed, you're wrong ...

Here's what you can do to help ...

If you want to talk about it ...

The sound of the wind made him nervous ...

"Why didn't you show up earlier?" she asked ...

I wanted to finish the job, but ...

Here's what you need to know ...

What can make a difference ...

It was the first time she had ever ridden a horse ...

What happened that day would change everything ...

Here's what I didn't know ...

All it takes is ...

I closed my eyes, and this is what I saw ...

Here's why I think everyone should _____ ...

Here's what no one can take away from me ...

"Why can't you people stop bothering me?"

When I packed for the trip to Mars, here's what I brought ...

If you'd just listen, you might learn something ...

I know you're busy, but I need your help ...

Because I'm your friend, I'm going to tell you ...

In the middle of the night, thunder began to rumble ...

The path led deeper into the forest ...

He wished for the world to be different ...

I did everything I could ...

Thanks!

This writing book couldn't have happened without a lot of help and creativity. Thanks first of all to my amazing partner and Write Mondays co-founder Deb Fleischman, an amazing writer and teacher and the person who first wondered what would happen if we gave kids 7-Minute Prompts. I also want to thank the incredible Bess O-Brien, documentary filmmaker extraordinaire, who invited me to teach writing to people recovering from addiction. The result was Writers for Recovery, which for the past six years has helped people of all ages and backgrounds to use writing as a healing force.

I wouldn't know anything about writing without my teachers. First among these is Rick Simpson, my poetry teacher at St. Bonaventure University, who first convinced me I had a talent worth exploring. In grad school at Vermont College of Fine Arts, I was blessed to have some amazing teachers and mentors. Thanks to Diane Lefer, Pamela Painter, Christopher Noël, and Douglas Glover for sharing their knowledge and wisdom with me. Doug's excellent book on technique *Attack of the Copula Spiders* and Pam's book of writing exercises *What If?* are treasures to the writing community and much recommended. They were both big influences on this book.

Thanks to my team of writing "cousins," who I count on to guide me in this crazy process: Sandra Miller, Lisa Carey, John "Po" Powers, and the late great Tom Miller. I couldn't have done it without you. I am grateful also to my editorial colleagues in Boston, including the late Judy Cooper, Rennie Boy, Ann Reckner, and others too numerous to include here. You took pity on me when I knew nothing about writing and helped me grow.

Finally, I would like to thank Rob Madrick, Peder Jones, and Liam Spalding, who made critical contributions to my final edit.

I am grateful to you all.

Gary

About the Author

Gary Miller is a writer, editor, and teacher living in Vermont. He has worked as a developmental editor of K-12 educational materials for over 20 years. A graduate of Vermont College of Fine Arts, Gary is the author of the short story collection *Museum of the Americas* (Fomite Press), which was a finalist for the Vermont Book Award. His documentary film script writing work has earned him three New England Emmy Award nominations. He is a partner, the dad of one amazing kid, and the stepdad of another. And he's a fly fisherman who's still trying to get it right.

www.ingramcontent.com/pod-product-compliance
Lightning Source LLC
Chambersburg PA
CBHW072016060426
42446CB00043B/2635